THE WAY
OF THE WOLF

THE GOSPEL IN NEW IMAGES

The Way
of the Wolf
The Gospel in New Images

Martin Bell

A CROSSROAD BOOK

THE SEABURY PRESS

NEW YORK

The New Testament quotations on pp. 121–128 are from
The New English Bible, copyright © 1961 by the
Delegates of the Oxford University Press and the Syndics
of the Cambridge University Press.

Eleventh Printing
Copyright © 1968, 1969, 1970 by Martin Bell
ISBN: 0-8164-0202-7
Library of Congress Catalog Card Number: 77-120366
Design by Carol Basen

Printed in the United States of America

For My Father

Contents

THE WAY
OF THE WOLF

THE GOSPEL IN NEW IMAGES

Barrington Bunny

ONCE upon a time in a large forest there lived a very furry bunny. He had one lop ear, a tiny black nose, and unusually shiny eyes. His name was Barrington.

Barrington was not really a very handsome bunny. He was brown and speckled and his ears didn't stand up right. But he could hop, and he was, as I have said, very furry.

In a way, winter is fun for bunnies. After all, it gives them an opportunity to hop in the snow and then turn around to see where they have hopped. So, in a way, winter was fun for Barrington.

But in another way winter made Barrington sad. For, you see, winter marked the time when all of the animal families got together in their cozy homes to celebrate Christmas. He could hop, and he was very furry. But as far as Barrington knew, he was the only bunny in the forest.

When Christmas Eve finally came, Barrington did not feel like going home all by himself. So he decided that he would hop for awhile in the clearing in the center of the forest.

Hop. Hop. Hippity-hop. Barrington made tracks in the fresh snow.

Hop. Hop. Hippity-hop. Then he cocked his head and looked back at the wonderful designs he had made.

"Bunnies," he thought to himself, "can hop. And they are very warm, too, because of how furry they are."

(But Barrington didn't really know whether or not this was true of all bunnies, since he had never met another bunny.)

When it got too dark to see the tracks he was making, Barrington made up his mind to go home.

On his way, however, he passed a large oak tree. High in the branches there was a great deal of excited chattering going on. Barrington looked up. It was a squirrel family! What a marvelous time they seemed to be having.

"Hello, up there," called Barrington.

"Hello, down there," came the reply.

"Having a Christmas party?" asked Barrington.

"Oh, yes!" answered the squirrels. "It's Christmas Eve. Everybody is having a Christmas party!"

"May I come to your party?" said Barrington softly.

"Are you a squirrel?"

"No."

"What are you, then?"

"A bunny."

"A bunny?"

"Yes."

"Well, how can you come to the party if you're a bunny? Bunnies can't climb trees."

"That's true," said Barrington thoughtfully. "But I can hop and I'm very furry and warm."

"We're sorry," called the squirrels. "We don't know anything about hopping and being furry, but we do know that in order to come to our house you have to be able to climb trees."

"Oh, well," said Barrington. "Merry Christmas."

"Merry Christmas," chattered the squirrels.

And the unfortunate bunny hopped off toward his tiny house.

It was beginning to snow when Barrington reached the river. Near the river bank was a wonderfully constructed house of sticks and mud. Inside there was singing.

"It's the beavers," thought Barrington. "Maybe they will let me come to their party."

And so he knocked on the door.

"Who's out there?" called a voice.

"Barrington Bunny," he replied.

There was a long pause and then a shiny beaver head broke the water.

"Hello, Barrington," said the beaver.

"May I come to your Christmas party?" asked Barrington.

The beaver thought for awhile and then he said, "I suppose so. Do you know how to swim?"

"No," said Barrington, "but I can hop and I am very furry and warm."

"Sorry," said the beaver. "I don't know anything about hopping and being furry, but I do know that in order to come to our house you have to be able to swim."

"Oh, well," Barrington muttered, his eyes filling with tears. "I suppose that's true—Merry Christmas."

"Merry Christmas," called the beaver. And he disappeared beneath the surface of the water.

Even being as furry as he was, Barrington was beginning to get cold. And the snow was falling so hard that his tiny, bunny eyes could scarcely see what was ahead of him.

He was almost home, however, when he heard the excited squeaking of field mice beneath the ground.

"It's a party," thought Barrington. And suddenly he blurted out through his tears, "Hello, field mice. This is Barrington Bunny. May I come to your party?"

But the wind was howling so loudly and Barrington was sobbing so much that no one heard him.

And when there was no response at all, Barrington just sat down in the snow and began to cry with all his might.

"Bunnies," he thought, "aren't any good to anyone. What good is it to be furry and to be able to hop if you don't have any family on Christmas Eve?"

Barrington cried and cried. When he stopped crying he began to bite on his bunny's foot, but he did not move from where he was sitting in the snow.

Suddenly, Barrington was aware that he was not alone. He looked up and strained his shiny eyes to see who was there.

To his surprise he saw a great silver wolf. The wolf was large and strong and his eyes flashed fire. He was the most beautiful animal Barrington had ever seen.

For a long time the silver wolf didn't say anything at all. He just stood there and looked at Barrington with those terrible eyes.

Then slowly and deliberately the wolf spoke. *(Pause)* "Barrington," he asked in a gentle voice, "why are you sitting in the snow?"

"Because it's Christmas Eve," said Barrington, "and I don't have any family, and bunnies aren't any good to anyone."

"Bunnies are, too, good," said the wolf. "Bunnies can hop and they are very warm."

"What good is that?" Barrington sniffed.

"It is very good indeed," the wolf went on, "because it is a gift that bunnies are given, a free gift with no strings attached. And every gift that is given to anyone is given for a reason. Someday you will see why it is good to hop and to be warm and furry."

"But it's Christmas," moaned Barrington, "and I'm all alone. I don't have any family at all."

"Of course you do," replied the great silver wolf. "All of the animals in the forest are your family."

And then the wolf disappeared. He simply wasn't there. Barrington had only blinked his eyes, and when he looked—the wolf was gone.

"All of the animals in the forest are my family," *slow* thought Barrington. "It's good to be a bunny. Bunnies can hop. That's a gift." And then he said it again. "A gift. A free gift."

On into the night Barrington worked. First he found the best stick that he could. (And that was difficult because of the snow.)

Then hop. Hop. Hippity-hop. To beaver's house. He left the stick just outside the door. With a note on it that read: "Here is a good stick for your house. It is a gift. A free gift. No strings attached. Signed, a member of your family."

"It is a good thing that I can hop," he thought, "because the snow is very deep."

Then Barrington dug and dug. Soon he had gathered together enough dead leaves and grass to make the squirrels' nest warmer. Hop. Hop. Hippity-hop.

He laid the grass and leaves just under the large oak tree and attached this message: "A gift. A free gift. From a member of your family."

It was late when Barrington finally started home. And what made things worse was that he knew a blizzard was beginning.

Hop. Hop. Hippity-hop.

Soon poor Barrington was lost. The wind howled furiously, and it was very, very cold. "It certainly is cold," he said out loud. "It's a good thing I'm so furry. But if I don't find my way home pretty soon even I might freeze!"

Squeak. Squeak. . . .

And then he saw it—a baby field mouse lost in the snow. And the little mouse was crying.

"Hello, little mouse," Barrington called.

"Don't cry. I'll be right there." Hippity-hop, and Barrington was beside the tiny mouse.

"I'm lost," sobbed the little fellow. "I'll never find my way home, and I know I'm going to freeze."

"You won't freeze," said Barrington. "I'm a bunny and bunnies are very furry and warm. You stay right where you are and I'll cover you up."

Barrington lay on top of the little mouse and hugged him tight. The tiny fellow felt himself surrounded by warm fur. He cried for awhile but soon, snug and warm, he fell asleep.

Barrington had only two thoughts that long, cold night. First he thought, "It's good to be a bunny. Bunnies are very furry and warm." And then, when he felt the heart of the tiny mouse beneath him beating regularly, he thought, "All of the animals in the forest are my family."

Next morning, the field mice found their little boy, asleep in the snow, warm and snug beneath the furry carcass of a dead bunny. Their relief and excitement was so great that they didn't even think to question where the bunny had come from.

And as for the beavers and the squirrels, they still wonder which member of their family left the little gifts for them that Christmas Eve.

After the field mice had left, Barrington's frozen body simply lay in the snow. There was no sound except that of the howling wind. And no one anywhere in the forest noticed the great silver wolf who came to stand beside that brown, lop-eared carcass.

But the wolf did come.

And he stood there.
Without moving or saying a word.
All Christmas Day.
Until it was night.
And then he disappeared into the forest.

THE SECRET OF THE STARS

Who could have dreamed that this lit - tle ba - by —

Here in the man - ger, cry - ing for his mom - ma —

Who could have dreamed that this lit - tle ba - by — Would

change the course of the world? — All too soon he'll be

leav - ing his mom - ma. — Strid - ing a - long by the

banks of the ri - ver. — Call - ing to fish - er - men who

Words and music copyright © 1968 by Martin Bell

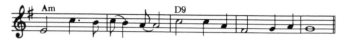

fol - low, be - wild - ered. _ Chang - ing the course of the world.

CHORUS

The stars shine bright.   What do they know?   Is there a

se - cret they keep?   O Ho - ly Night.   The child shi- vers

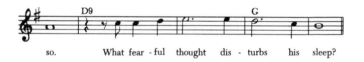

so.   What fear - ful thought dis - turbs his sleep?

Could it be the same lit - tle ba - by __ All a - lone and

fast - ing in the des - ert?_While all a- round the coun-try- side his

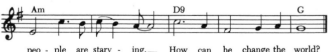

peo - ple are starv - ing. __ How can he change the world?

THE SECRET OF THE STARS

1. Who could have dreamed that this little baby
   Here in the manger, crying for his momma—
   Who could have dreamed that this little baby
   Would change the course of the world?

   All too soon he'll be leaving his momma.
   Striding along by the banks of the river.
   Calling to fishermen who follow, bewildered.
   Changing the course of the world.

   The stars shine bright.
   What do they know?
   Is there a secret they keep?
   O Holy Night. The child shivers so.
   What fearful thought disturbs his sleep?

   Could it be the same little baby
   All alone and fasting in the desert?
   While all about the countryside his people are
      starving.
   How can he change the world?

2. Is this my child surrounded by people?
   Walking with men who wish they'd never met him!
   Is this my baby? And how can they believe him?
   How can he change the world?

   Another village. Another crowd of people.
   High on a hill, he's preaching like a madman.
   If he doesn't stop, I swear they're going to kill him.
   He can't change the world.

   The stars shine bright.
   What do they know?
   Is there a secret they keep?
   O Holy Night. The child shivers so.
   What fearful thought disturbs his sleep?

   The time will come when he'll ride into the city
   Though all his friends say to stay out on the moun-
       tain.
   Riding alone. Shattering illusion.
   Changing the course of the world.

3. Hush-a-bye, go to sleep little baby
   Here in the manger, safe beside your momma.
   Only the angels who watch as you're sleeping
   Know that you'll change the world.

   And tonight the silent stars behold him.
   Shining their brightest to try to keep from crying.
   Did they guess? Or have the angels told them
   The price of changing the world?

The stars shine bright.
What do they know?
Is there a secret they keep?
O Holy Night. The child shivers so.
What fearful thought disturbs his sleep?

Today other mommas are holding their children.
Children who'll grow up and follow where he
   leads them.
God have mercy, and comfort all the mommas
Of children who change the world.

Noel—
The
Lone Ranger

I. Israel.
   The chosen people of God.
   The elect.
   Singled out.
   To be a light to the Nations.
   Israel.
   How odd that God should choose the Jews . . .

> Thus says the Lord God: On the day when I chose Israel, I swore to the seed of the house of Jacob, making myself known to them in the land of Egypt, I swore to them, saying, I am the Lord your God. On that day I swore to them that I would bring them out of the land of Egypt into a land that I had searched out for them, a land flowing with milk and honey, the most glorious of all lands.

Israel.
The broken people of God.
The hungry.
The captive.
The persecuted.

The dispersed.
The despised.
People of God.

> And the haughtiness of man shall be hum-
> bled and the pride of men shall be
> brought low, and God alone will be ex-
> alted in that day!

The people of God.
Enslaved by the Egyptians.
Crushed by the Assyrians.
Broken by the Babylonians.
Desecrated by the Greeks.
Tyrannized by the Romans.
Exterminated by the Germans.
Despised by the Nations.
Israel.
The chosen people of God.
The elect.
Singled out.
To be a light to the Nations.
How odd that God should choose the Jews . . .
And the world groans under an unbearable bur-
    den.
Like a woman in childbirth the world cries out.
The world in captivity.
The world in chains.
And Israel—
The chosen people of God—
In chains.
There is no deliverance. But God.

Come Emmanuel.
Ransom captive Israel.
Emmanuel.
Mighty God.
Everlasting Father.
Prince of Peace.
Deliver Israel.
That Israel might be a light to the Nations.
But no . . .

II. The Magi.
Wise men.
Orientals.
Foreigners.
Waiting.
Pacing back and forth.
Expecting.
Charting the heavens.
Waiting for a sign.
Perhaps a star.
Surely a star.
At least a star!
The Wise Men are uneasy.
And then it happens.
The really wise men know.
It has happened.

And they travel through the vast deserts of their living rooms on slow-moving newspaper headlines that scream. It has happened!

U.P.I. Oklahoma City.
Guess what?
A baby was born on a downtown sidewalk.
In the snow.
While people hurried on by.
All alone.
Except for the disinterested glance of
>   A taxicab driver.
>   A politician.
>   A salesman.
>   And a few hundred other people.

All alone.
A mother screaming for help.
A newborn infant shivering in the cold.
And an unnoticed star appearing in the West.
Over Oklahoma City.
In the U.S.A.
In the Western Hemisphere.
In the World.
In the Universe.
In the mind of God.
The Magi.
Wise Men.
Orientals.
Foreigners.
Pacing back and forth.
Waiting.

For an astronaut to return from outer space with a very funny story. The funny story goes like this:

The astronaut has been out in space.

And everyone is waiting for his report on whether or not he has seen God. Now this is the funny part. Hold on now. Here's the punch line.

He returns.

And he has seen God.

And they ask him to describe God.

And he says: (This is it!)

"God—She's a Negro!"

You see why it's funny, don't you?

She's black.

III. Israel.

The chosen people of God.

The elect.

Singled out.

To be a light to the Nations.

Israel.

How odd that God should choose the blacks.

And then God manifested himself—revealed himself

As an outlaw.

A fugitive from justice.

He was masked.

No one.

No one!

Knew who he was.

Not even his disciples.
Although they had glimpsed behind the mask.
They still didn't know him.
He came unto his own and they knew him not.
Foxes have holes.
Birds have their nests.
But the Son of Man has nowhere to lay his head.
There used to be a television program about
    him.
It was called—*The Fugitive.*
There was no way to know who he was.
There is no way to know who he is.
Except by signs.
And these are the signs by which you will rec-
    ognize him . . .
He will not look like God.
He will be masked.
There will be no room for him in the world.
A silver bullet will tell more about him than his
    appearance.
Wherever he goes nothing will ever be the same
    again.
Only after he has gone will anyone realize who
    has been there.
And in the end he will die in order that we might
    live.
His name is legion.
His face is masked.
Only very wise men and children will ever rec-
    ognize him.
And he is here today. Because

You
Are the Christ.
The chosen one.
The broken one.
The one who is ripped apart and torn into shreds
      and scattered
      and dispersed
      and despised
      and chained. . . .
This is your mask.
Surprised? You should be.
Unbelieving? Naturally.
Frightened? I should hope so.
Don't be afraid—I am bringing you glad tidings
   of great joy.
For out of you this day the Christ is born.
God loves you.
Amen.
Don't be afraid.
Amen.
It's good to be as broken as you are.
Amen.
Be nice to each other.
Amen.
It's good to be you.
Amen.

What the Wind Said to Thajir

ONCE upon a time there was a little boy whose name was Thajir. Thajir liked the sunshine, and he especially liked the grass and trees, but his favorite thing in all the world was wind. Whenever there was wind, Thajir would run to get his hat and coat, and then when he was all bundled up, he would go for a walk.

One day when Thajir was out walking, the wind said hello to him. Naturally he was very surprised. He had heard the wind many times before. But it had never said hello to him. Thajir pulled up the ear flaps on his fuzzy hat and sat down beside a fir tree to listen. This is what the wind said:

"Thajir, you are my friend. I would like to tell you something important. Please listen carefully and try to remember what I say. Regardless of what anyone else may ever tell you, regardless even of what your own experience may lead you to believe, everything that is, is good. At the center of things, life belongs to life. Do you think you can remember that, Thajir?"

The little boy nodded his head. "Everything that is, is good," he said. "And at the center of things, life belongs to life."

The wind whistled softly. "Thajir, you are my friend. I have told you a great secret. Would you like to hear more?"

Thajir smiled and hugged his knees. "Yes, indeed!" he said out loud. He was glad that the wind was talking to him.

"All right then, here is another secret that is almost as important as the first: regardless of what anyone else may ever tell you, regardless even of what your own experience may lead you to believe, you are everyone who ever was and everyone who ever will be. You are the whole of creation—past, present, and future. Decisions that you make today, in what is called the here and the now, will validate or invalidate everything that has gone before, and make possible or impossible everything that is to come. Anything that hurts anyone, hurts you. Anything that helps anyone, helps you. It is not possible to gain from another's loss, or to lose from another's gain. Your life is immensely important. Everything depends upon you. Thajir, do you understand this, or is it too difficult?"

"Oh, it is not difficult at all!" the little boy replied. "You have said that I am everyone and everything. And because this is true, nothing can hurt anyone without hurting me, and nothing can help anyone without helping me. It is not difficult to understand. Please tell me more of your secrets!"

For a short time there was silence. It was as if the boy had surprised the wind with his answer.

"Thajir, you are my friend. I forgot momentarily

that you were a child, and it surprised me that you understood so quickly. I am not accustomed to such immediate insight. But then, usually I talk with grown-ups. I'm afraid it is much more difficult for grown-ups to understand what I have to say than it is for children. I am very pleased with you, Thajir. It is indeed rewarding to talk with someone who does not find my secrets difficult to understand."

Thajir smiled. He liked the wind. What other wonderful things would he learn today?

"There is something else," the wind went on, "something I have always hesitated to talk about with one so young. But you have called my hesitancy into question with your immediate apprehension of my most difficult secrets. Therefore, let us continue. Thajir, you are my friend. I would like you to know the formula that correlates all of existence with the origin and aim of life. It is my desire that you should grasp the most basic truth about historical existence, the principle of intentionality by means of which fate is transformed into meaningful destiny, despair is rendered powerless, and hopelessness is overcome by joy. Thajir, regardless of what anyone else may ever tell you, regardless even of what your own experience may lead you to believe, it is in dying that one lives. It is in losing one's life that he finds it. You must never fear dying, my little friend, because fear of dying leads one to all sorts of futile and demonic attempts to preserve life. And life simply cannot be preserved. Meaning and purpose are the correlates of sacrificial love. One is united with the origin and aim of life precisely as he expends himself on behalf of the entire world. It is a hard lesson to learn, but it is the most basic truth about historical existence. Is this clear? Perhaps I have gone too fast?"

Thajir's eyes were bright with excitement. "I couldn't understand all of the words," he said, "but I think I know what you mean. It is just as important as learning that everything that is, is good—that at the center of things, life belongs to life. It is much the same as understanding that I am everyone who ever was and everyone who ever will be. I do not know quite how to say it, but you have pointed out that I must not be afraid to die. On the contrary, you have said that the very meaning and purpose of life is grasped in the process of dying on behalf of the world. I suppose it is something like dying in order to give myself life. I mean, if I am everyone and everything—past, present and future—then it is not others who will live as a result of my expending my life in history. It is rather I myself who will live. Such an expanded view of myself as you have presented in your second great secret makes the conclusion of this most recent insight inescapable."

"Once again you have surprised me, Thajir," the wind whispered. "I am taken aback by your uncanny ability to seize upon the core of my teaching. You are indeed a magnificent child. But I wonder whether or not you will remember all of this when you are grown. It is conceivable that you will soon forget what I have said."

Thajir smiled and hugged his knees. "Will you

forget having talked with me?" he asked.

"No," the wind replied, "that would not be possible."

"Then neither will it be possible for me to forget what you have said," the little boy concluded.

Thajir sat quietly beside the fir tree for a length of time. When he was certain that the wind had gone, he pulled down the ear flaps on his fuzzy hat and started home.

That night, Thajir's mother read him a story about elephants. After she had finished reading the story, she asked him what he remembered about it.

Thajir said it was most important to remember that whatever hurt elephants hurt him, and that whatever helped elephants helped him. He added that at the center of things, life belonged to life, and this meant that he and elephants shared in the same experience and were somehow united with one another. He went on to say that it was good to be an elephant, and it was good to be Thajir.

Thajir's mother did not question what he had said. It was not the answer she had expected, but it was a fine answer. Being an exceedingly wise woman, she let it go at that, closed the book about elephants, and tucked Thajir into bed. For a moment she stared at the little boy who was already asleep.

"I'm afraid for him!" she said through unanticipated tears. "Oh God, I'm afraid for him! What will become of my Thajir?" Naturally, there was no reply. No sound at all inside the room. And outside, in the darkness, only the howling wind.

INCARNATUS

On - ly the lit - tle chil - dren Know what they are

look - ing for. They wan - der all a - long the streets and

look be - neath the cob - ble - stones; And I have wan - dered

al - so A - mong the man - y streets of life And

won - dered at the mys - ter - y and trem - bled in the

lone - ly night. _____ In a world ___ full of

mys - ter - y ___ How I long to be ___ like a new - born child. ___

See - ing _____ for the first time _____ What was al - ways there _

___ be - fore my eyes. ___ Now ___ to my sur - prise. ___

INCARNATUS

1. Only the little children
   Know what they are looking for.
   They wander all along the streets
   And look beneath the cobblestones;
   And I have wandered also
   Among the many streets of life
   And wondered at the mystery
   And trembled in the lonely night.

   In a world full of mystery
   How I long to be like a newborn child.
   Seeing for the first time
   What was always there before my eyes. Now to
   *   my surprise—*

2. I would see the angels
   Who guard the men who walk the street,
   And meet the gaze of those who say
   They have not had enough to eat.
   And recognize the splendor
   Of every whore who called my name.
   And I would know enough to show her
   She and I are just the same.

In a world full of mystery
How I long to be like a newborn child.
Seeing for the first time
What was always there before my eyes—that life
  belongs to life.

3. Drunken men who stand and laugh
   And will not ever live again.
   They're dead inside, but with my eyes
   I'd recognize the seraphim.
   And God himself, a drunken man
   Who's staggering inside the door.
   The Holy One of Israel,
   Mistaken for a broken whore.

In a world full of mystery
How I long to be like a newborn child.
Seeing for the first time
What was always there before my eyes—that life
  belongs to God.

Hunger
and
Hurricanes

TO be human is to be hungry. All children are hungry. They are born hungry. Most children are always hungry. Some children are starving. It is terrifying to see a starving child. It is more terrifying to be a starving child. Starvation is horrible. To be without food is hell.

To have experienced the Christ, to have encountered Jesus of Nazareth, to have run headlong into the person of God in the flesh must have been like stepping into the path of a hurricane. No one would do it intentionally. Human beings do not seek out hurricanes. Hurricanes happen. Suddenly. Often without much warning. If we can avoid "being there," we do. If we can't, we don't. It is really almost as simple as that. To experience the Christ is to run headlong into the path of a hurricane. Jesus said: Man cannot live by bread alone. He said that to hungry human beings. He said that to starving children. Yet, Jesus was criticized for eating with publicans and sinners, for going among the people eating and drinking, for being a winebibber, for eating grain on the Sabbath, for eating when he was hungry and sleeping when he was tired. He was criticized by hungry human beings. He was chastized by starving children.

On the other hand, for forty days and forty nights Jesus was without food. He told Martha that she was too concerned with food. He said: when you are without food, wash your face. He said: you are too worried about what you shall eat and what you shall drink. He sent his disciples out without food, and on the cross he refused a sponge filled with vinegar and hyssop.

Jesus ate and drank. And he didn't eat and drink. He was something of a paradox as regards hunger and fulfillment. Curiously enough, what has been called the extension of the Body of Christ—the Church—eats and drinks and it doesn't eat and drink. The Church feasts. And the Church fasts. The central act of the Church is a common meal. The ultimate mythical fulfillment of the Church is a heavenly banquet. The Church is something of a paradox as regards hunger and fulfillment.

To be human is to be hungry. Most children are always hungry. Some children are starving. Starvation is horrible. To be without food is hell.

To be the Christ, to be Jesus of Nazareth, to be the person of God incarnate must be like being the eye of a hurricane. The eye of a hurricane is its focus, its power, the apparently unmoving force that instigates the terrible headwind. The hurricane's eye is self-contained and calm. Yet the experience of the hurricane itself is scattering, disassembling, chaotic, violent motion.

The action of God in history is something of a paradox. One of our hymns reflects this disturbing paradox when it says:

The peace of God—it is no peace—but
strife sown in the sod. . . .

St. Peter appears to have found the peace of God in an upside-down cross. Human beings do not intentionally seek out upside-down crosses. Upside-down crosses happen. Suddenly. Often without warning. If we can avoid "being there" we do. If we can't, we don't. It is really almost as simple as that.

God's action in history is something of a paradox as regards hunger and fulfillment. Is it true that 5,000 people who have run headlong into the path of a hurricane and who are hungry for food and starving for peace can have their hunger sated, their very guts which have been torn apart healed? And if it is conceivable, can it happen through the vehicles of a few fish, a little bread, and a Word? Frankly, I don't know. But I can't say that I don't care, because I do. I care terribly. After all, I'm very hungry. And I am caught in the headwind of a hurricane.

Christ have mercy upon me.

And Jesus had compassion upon the 5,000 for he saw that they had been with him the whole day and were very hungry.

Lord have mercy upon me.

And so he asked a little boy (who else?) to share his food with them. And from the hands of a child they were fed. Children are nice. Jesus likes children.

Christ have mercy upon me.

Starvation is horrible. To be without food is hell.

Maranatha. Lord come.

Human beings do not seek out hurricanes. Hurricanes happen.

Lord now lettest thou thy servant depart in peace.

And because Jesus had compassion upon them, and because a little boy had some fish, and because the eye of the hurricane enveloped them, they ate and were filled and went home. It was not very spectacular, but then, what is? It appears that Jesus simply left it at that. And then he took a deep breath of fresh air and went back to being a fugitive.

Amen.

Where Are the Nine?

HOW about a word or two on behalf of the nine lepers who did not return to give thanks? The gospel reads something like this: there were ten lepers cleansed and one of them—just one of them—when he saw that he was healed, turned back and in a loud voice glorified God and fell down on his face at Jesus' feet, giving him thanks.

And Jesus answering said, "Were there not ten cleansed? But where are the nine?"

Ten lepers were cleansed and one of them returned to give thanks. That must be a nice thing to be able to do.

What about the others? It's simple, really. One of them was frightened—that's all. He didn't understand what had happened, and it frightened him. So he looked for some place to hide. Jesus scared him.

A second was offended because he had not been required to do something difficult before he could be healed. It was all too easy. He had expected months, maybe years, of fasting and prayer and washing and righteous living to be the requirement. But he had done none of this. He had not earned his reward. His motto was "you get what you pay for." And so Jesus offended him.

The third had realized too late that he had not really wanted to be cleansed. That he did not know what to do or how to live or even who he was without his leprosy. Although it had been his fervent plea to be healed, he now began to see how much he had needed his leprosy and consequently how necessary it had been in defining him as a person. Jesus had taken away his identity.

It is difficult to explain the reason why the fourth leper did not return to give thanks. Perhaps because it is such a simple reason—and perhaps because we very nearly tread on holy ground even to talk about it. In a word, the fourth leper did not return because in his delirium of joy, he forgot. He forgot. That's all. He was so happy that he forgot.

The fifth leper was unable to say thank you any more to anybody. There is something that happens to a man who must beg and who is shunned by his fellows, and who is grudgingly thrown a few coins and who is always—in the midst of such an existence and in the face of such treatment (perhaps even because of such treatment, for instance, the few coins) —expected to say thank you. He just doesn't say thank you any more to anybody—not even to Jesus.

The sixth leper was a woman—a mother who had been separated from her family for eleven years because of the leprosy. She was now free to rejoin her husband and children. She did not return to give thanks because she was hurrying home. Like a wild animal released from captivity, she had been freed by Jesus. And like the animal, she simply went straight home.

The seventh just didn't believe that Jesus had anything to do with the cleansing. He knew that healing had taken place, but why and how were the questions. Certainly he did not believe in hocus pocus, magic, miracles—any of that. There was a perfectly intelligible explanation of what had happened, but it didn't have anything to do with Jesus. He didn't return to give thanks because Jesus had had nothing to do with the healing event.

The eighth leper did not return precisely because he did believe that Jesus had healed him—that the Kingdom of God was here and the Messiah had arrived. To return to give thanks when the Kingdom of God was so close at hand—unheard of! And so he ran to publish the news.

What shall I say about the ninth leper? What was his experience? Why didn't he return? I don't know the answer to either of these questions. All I know is that he showed himself to the priest and immediately was cleansed. He then stood still for a moment and smiled. The priest reports that the ninth leper gave two utterances. First he said, "So!" And then, "Ah, yes!" Without another word he walked away. His eyes blazed fire but his shoulders sagged as if under a great burden. The air around him was silent. Then without warning he turned his head suddenly and fixed his eyes upon a rock by the side of the road. "Hah!" he screamed. And you can make of this what you will, but the priest says that the rock actually jumped a foot off the ground. The ninth leper then said, "So!" and "Ah, yes!" and disappeared from sight. It is impossible to say precisely why he did not return to give thanks.

Ten were cleansed and only one returned. It must be nice to be able to do that. What shall I say now—that the real point is not that one returned but that ten were cleansed? You already know that. That condemnation is easier than investigation—that if we take time to investigate the reasons why people act as they do, we would find that they have to act the way they do and that such action in the light of the circumstances is quite understandable and totally forgivable and even completely reasonable and just as it should be? You already know that.

What then shall I say? That it is good to give thanks? Yes. That it is understandable not to give thanks? Yes. That God does not heal people and then stand around just waiting for us to say thank you and then get angry and have his feelings hurt if we don't? Yes, that's true. Which is the same thing as saying—no, he certainly doesn't.

But what of the nine? They are on the way home, hiding in fear, refusing to believe, offended at what they call cheap grace, so happy they forgot, lost without their leprosy, unable to say thank you ever again, publishing the news of the coming of the King-dom—God, who knows where they are! The point is this: Jesus does. He knows where they are. First he says to the leper who did return, "Arise, go thy way," and then he goes his own way—with a strange smile on his lips. But where are the nine? Don't you see it in his eyes? He knows where they are. He knew all along. Without another word Jesus walks away. His eyes blaze fire but his shoulders sag as if under a great burden. The air around him is silent. Then without warning he turns his head suddenly and fixes his eyes upon a rock by the side of the road. "Hah!" he screams. And you can make out of this what you will, but they say the rock actually jumped a foot off the ground. Jesus then said, "So!" and "Ah, yes!" and disappeared from sight.

It is impossible to say precisely why Jesus did not return to give thanks.

How the Demons Captured Amy and What Happened Then

AMY Pembington had never seen a demon. Nor did demonic elements occupy any part whatsoever in her wider life experience. Not as far as she knew anyway. Perhaps that is why she was so indignant when Lena, the Gypsy woman, told her that no less than seven virulent demons of almost unbelievable proportion and magnitude presently inhabited her person.

She should have known better than to consult the Gypsy. Fortunetelling and tarot cards, magic tricks and mumbo jumbo—what insanity! Surely she had gotten what she deserved. If a person insists on consulting fortunetellers, then she must expect to hear such nonsense. Amy let her fingers stray across the textured fabric of Lena's faded tablecloth. The pungency of incense and perfume, stale smoke and human warmth. The room was stifling.

Amy Pembington sat carefully with her attractive legs crossed at the ankles. On first encounter, one might say that she was somewhere in her late twenties. Soon, however, it would become clear that the initial impression had more to do with choice of clothing, makeup and hair style than with chronology. It would be safe to say that this strikingly handsome woman was at least thirty-five years of age, maybe even forty. To be more precise, one might add that it would be safe to say this to anyone except Amy Pembington.

On the evening in question, Amy had chosen to wear her tailored, wool suit with the skirt that ended abruptly at mid-thigh. The dark, seamless nylon hose lended an aura of enchantment to her almost perfect legs. Hardly unaware of the profound effect of such malevolence on the men and women trapped within her sphere of influence, Amy complemented this ensemble with a pale opaque lipstick and matching lacquered nails. Coiffed to nearly unattainable perfection, her gleaming, scented hair invited havoc. Seven virulent demons, Lena had said. Seven sneering parasites of almost unbelievable magnitude and proportion. Foolishness.

One cut of the tarot cards and then: the hangedman, symbol of selfishness. Amy closed her eyes and let her mind run free. What was it Paul had said? Was it that he loved her, or that he would soon return from Terre Haute? No matter. God, what turgid, unrelenting boredom he could offer. Why had she not left him long ago? The candle on the table flickered slightly and the Gypsy woman moaned aloud. The sound made Amy's shoulders contract as in pain. What curious torque of reasoning had brought her to this place? The whole bizarre event unfolding here within these walls gave her the creeps. Now Lena spoke again.

"I see that you do not believe what I have said

about the demons." The Gypsy hag was grinning now—a toothless grin that was at very least unsettling to her guest. "Could it be that you imagine creatures that have scales and eyes of fire? Is it possible you think I speak of monsters from the pit with thrashing tails and jaws that close upon our inner parts like steel? Do not be such a child! I am not playing parlour games with you. To have consulted Lena is to have asked to hear the truth. Do not be so stupid. I am neither frivolous nor mad. I am a witch."

Amy closed her hand, but then, when the telltale veins stood out like tiny rivers, she corrected this mistake and opened it once again. Incense stronger now. A second tarot card: the woman, symbol of mystery. Once more, Lena's voice.

"I do not speak of creatures from the pit with eyes of fire. Not at all. I mean rather to indicate the facile and deceptive structures of illusion that imbed themselves inside the souls of men with such a vengeance as to take possession of their very lives. The seven virulent demons that are inhabiting you are not grotesque little monsters with thrashing tails. They are illusions, stories you are telling yourself that are utterly fallacious; bizarre and fantastic lies which you nevertheless believe, and which consequently are taking your life away from you. To have consulted Lena is to have asked to hear the truth. I have told you that I am a witch, and now I am going to show you something of my power."

A distortion in Lena's countenance. The candle brighter than before. Unwittingly, Amy Pembing-

ton's hand trembled. Then a third tarot card. Amy
would not look at it. Lena moaned and turned all
three cards face down on the table. Amy's composure
was beginning to crack. It was time to leave. She
should never have come here. What was happening?
Why was the room so small? The candle so huge?
Amy did not remember such a large candle. For a
moment she believed she was going to be sick. Then
everything came together. The room, the Gypsy hag,
the tarot cards and the candle all came into focus.
Amy's visual perception had returned. But now
Lena's voice spoke to her from echo chambers buried
in her mind.

"Amy, you are forty-three years old. It is time
now for you to learn the truth about yourself. You
cannot hide forever behind your striking beauty. Nor
will short skirts and seamless nylon hose protect you
from becoming what you see before your eyes, a
frail and toothless hag whose days are nearly over
with and done. Do not be deceived. You cannot
cheat the process of decay. It is a demon that pos-
sesses you and bids you hide from wrinkles and from
veins that stand out boldly on your hands. How do
you plan escape from death? Come now, Amy Pembington, it is an illusion to imagine you are twenty-
four. It is time now to grow up."

Somewhere deep inside, Amy felt a shattering.
A ripping and a tearing in her guts. Was it Lena
moaning, or had she made that awful sound? The
candle moved from side to side, and Lena's eyes
rolled backwards in her head.

"The second of the demons is yet stronger than the first. A bargaining with idolatry that results in nothing short of aimless drifting, falsely labeled 'life.' It is a story you have told yourself for years. It is a fable of the if and then. If only this, then that. If only it were summer, then you could be happy. If only you were there instead of here. If only it were then instead of now. Hypothesis contrary to fact. Utterly illusional. Totally demonic. A wishful dreaming that robs one of the only reality ever available—the here and the now. Amy Pembington, to say you could be happy if it were summer is an absolutely meaningless statement! It is not summer. It is winter. There is no way in the world to make it summer. And so, if you are going to be happy, it will have to be happiness-in-winter. The only other choice you have is to coast, idle and drift aimlessly in the power of the demonic if and then."

Her breathing labored now, the Gypsy hag went on. "And so to the stubborn demons that surround your thinking about Paul, who is your husband. What are your words to describe his love? Turgid, unrelenting boredom. The folly is complete. The demons have their way. They turn your liquid reason into stone. The three of them are brothers. They are called Security, Freedom-in-Security, and Someday-Love-Will-Come. Paul cannot give you security, because there is no such thing beneath the sun to give. All security is illusion. It is a demon that bids you follow this bright path. And at the end, what can there be except the full anxiety of that which is: the insecure? And if what is, is insecure, how then a freedom that's secure? What kind of freedom would you have? This tentative and timid venturing forth that claims to circumvent all risk? Come out of her, you dog of hell! How long have you resided in her breast? And did you think forever to escape the judgment? Hurry now, be gone!

"Then finally to you, my cunning Someday-Love-Will-Come. Amy Pembington, do not stop now. The tally is not in. You must not move or break the spell. This night will yet determine all, the everything that is to be. So do not grow afraid or turn to run. When Lena speaks, the demons must obey. But Someday-Love-Will-Come is hiding still. Perhaps he dreams that Lena will go home and let him stay within your darkest inner place. What words can possibly describe this most voluptuous of deceits who builds his nest in drudgery. Should it be said that this one feasts on all the simple daily facts of human life—the disappointment and the boredom and the pain? The modest pleasures, what are they against such odds? Ah, someday love will come! My precious Amy, love is here. What you are dreaming of has never been, and it will never be. The cheap illusion of romance cannot suffice. You must be free from passion's twisted promise of enchantment later on. The staff of life is here within your grasp. Your love is Paul. Can you not see? Or are you blind?"

Amy's lovely features in contortion now. Her clothes in disarray. The perspiration glistened on her brow. One further movement of her arms. A futile, desperate supplicating glance and then, as if by chance, a slackening of the muscles in her face. And on the table, barely visible at all, the tiny candle sputtered its reply.

"So, they are gone," the Gypsy whispered to the air. "Five dark and ghoulish monsters from the pit; or should I say illusions, foul purveyors of the lie. I-Shall-Not-Die, the If-and-Then, Security, Freedom-In-Security, and Someday-Love-Will-Come. Their power is tremendous, these facile and deceptive structures of despair. But I have told you of my own strengths, and the witchcraft you have seen must serve to verify the mad, outrageous claims that I have made.

"Amy Pembington, be still. Two other demons lurk within the caverns of your soul. We dare not stop until the whole of this disease has been erased. Are you surprised by my persistence? Good. Then let us exorcise the two remaining lies that feed upon your heart. The first is not uncommon. Yet one dares not hope to penetrate its crusted armor quite so swiftly as before. Insidious and tepid parasite! This demon is called Things-Will-Soon-Work-Out. It has entirely to do with one's point of view, and its strength lies in the incontrovertible truth that time heals many wounds. To say that time heals many wounds, however, is not by any means to say things-will-soon-work-out. The lazy, mindless wandering encouraged by such a posited benevolence results in more destructive interaction among peoples than all the arguing and fighting in the world. It is not the case that things-will-soon-work-out. Ordinarily, things work out in direct relation to the amount of effort expended by the parties involved. This is a hard saying, but it is the truth, and as such must be respected. Amy Pembington, did you really believe that things-would-soon-work-out?"

A shifting of the tarot cards and then, "What shall I say to call the seventh demon out? Will it be enough to speak his name, or shall I tell about the grand deception that he perpetrates beneath a cloak of indignation and of seeking help? Such a fine up-standing lie! One almost shudders to betray so excellent a masking of reality. Is there not at least a grain of truth in the idea that my-life-has-to-do-with-other-people? Must I take responsibility for everything that happens in my world? Is it not possible to blame other people for many of my problems? Is there no such thing as turning to other people for help? Amy Pembington, listen to me! Your life is all about you. It is a demon that seeks to place responsibility for your life in the hands of someone else. It is a splendidly deceitful demon, but a demon all the same. And there is no reason for even so magnificent an illusion in your life, so long as you are living on the realistic level."

Once again a distortion in Amy's countenance. For a moment Amy had a sensation of falling. Inside her left shoulder an explosion. Then silence. The candle had gone out. Everything the same. The room. The faded tablecloth. The toothless Gypsy hag. What was different? Amy twisted in her chair.

The tarot cards were there face down before her. The scent of incense and perfume. Nothing had changed but Amy Pembington herself.

The old woman bent forward in her chair. "Are the demons gone?" she asked hesitantly.

"I don't know for sure," Amy said with a sudden shy, disarming smile, "but I believe they are."

"Good!" Lena replied. "That will be five dollars, please." The Gypsy hag stretched out her hand to take the bill. "I told you I was neither frivolous nor mad," she said and grinned her toothless grin. "I do not play parlour games, or gaze into a crystal ball. What I have told you is the truth. I am a witch."

Apparition

I

Alone now.
Quite alone.
Listening to the still,
       small sounds of the night.
Inhaling deeply from a phantom cigarette.
              Remembering too many
              other times when
      the smoke was real
And you were not
            an empty chair
            across the room.
A recollecting of perfume
      and warm, cream sherry wine.
A bitter chocolate corner
      of my mind
Where memory's faltering cadence
      wrestles free
From all my efforts to confine it to
            absurd and broken
               images.
              And so to have
     it be that which is
     over and done.

Over and done! What madness.
One might as well say
                   not begun
                   at all,
And offer himself meekly to
                   the sirens
                   in your place.
Fantastic, luminescent, smiling bitches all.
They speak of grace and hold up life's
                   creative,
                   ebullient facade.
As if somehow by
          an embrace
Ten thousand years of acquiescence
                   and of hate
Of starving children and embodied separation
Yet might fall.
The human race united in a kiss.
                   The wormwood and the gall
                   forgotten now.
Remember rather this,
A formula for proud and boisterous men,
          That living
                   we die.

II

Is that then how it ends,
With no hint of betrayal
                   or despair?
These antiseptic falterings pretend
                   to offer freedom.

It's a lie.

> Corrupt prevarications
>> hastily conceived!

Am I to hold their obscene bodies
> to my breast

And then believe the whispered teachings
>> they advance?

What kind of liberation shall I find
> within the trance
>> of such outrageous
>>> visions?

No.

I'd rather wait for you.

The solitary shelter of my room.

The memories. The lingering perfume.

> In retrospect one
> cannot help but smile.

My bold, adept enchantress without guile,
> how you have captured me!

Because of you, it is the truth alone
>> that satisfies my thirst.

A grappling with reality,

Confronting what at first would seem to
> bid me
>> build another wall around
>>> my inner parts.

Ingenious wench!

> You own my heart of hearts.

And imperceptibly your
> angular design

Has overcome the powers of
> benign,

indulgent
demons
who would lacerate my soul.
You speak the Word of life,
And by this Word
I am made whole.

III

Alone now.
Quite alone.
Listening to the still small sounds
of the night.
One further exposition brought to light.
A cherished pleasure that no longer dares to
hide.
My laconic willingness to seize
the wild, rebellious moment
And in spite of all, to
grieve with those who mourn,
To celebrate with those who laugh,
To groan with those who break beneath
the melancholy structures of
what is.
The whole responsive business of
my living in a world
of broken men.
The muted sound of violins.
A tambourine.
A swaying of the curtains that had been
quite still
before.

Have you returned, my evanescent,
          Gypsy love,
                    Or have I compensated
          with hallucination for
          the emptiness?
And what of this substrative, fearsome
                    urgency
                    I sense?
The interchange of restorative love
                    and of
          intense, somatic dissipation
                    that is mine.
Is this not just precisely where the line
          is drawn?
                    So what is real?
The present moment, or the
                    weary, listless nights
          when you are gone?
The answer is somewhere nearly in my
                    consciousness.
A sense of agitation and distress
                    brings me
                    to stumble from my chair.
          And there beside the
          curtain
          you should be.
But Christ, what is this apparition
          that I see!
No luminescent, smiling sirens in your place,
          Nor is it you, yourself who's come.
It is an awesome, dreadful face.

I turn to run
>   but cannot move
>   for fear.
In heaven's name, what does this mean?
There, across the room,
>   the empty chair,
And by its side,
>   I swear to God,
>   a snarling,
>   silver
>   wolf.

WALLS AND THINGS

I'm al - ways run - ning in - to walls and things. I

fall down a hun - dred times each day. But I'll

pick my - self up, Dust my - self off. I've de -

cid - ed that life is just that way.

CHORUS

And I cre - ate the world I live in _____ By

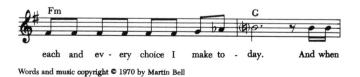

each and ev - ery choice I make to - day. And when

Words and music copyright © 1970 by Martin Bell

all is   said and done   I'm the on - ly   one   who can

make the   world a   bet - ter   place   to   stay.

WALLS AND THINGS

1. I'm always running into walls and things.
   I fall down a hundred times each day.
   But I'll pick myself up,
   Dust myself off.
   I've decided that life is just that way.

   [*chorus*]

   And I create the world I live in
   By each and every choice I make today.
   And when all is said and done
   I'm the only one
   Who can make the world
   A better place to stay.

2. I have a friend whose name is Mark,
   And Mark has a life that's just like mine.
   He often falls
      and he runs into walls.
   But Mark only laughs and says, "That's fine."

   [*chorus*]

   Because he creates the world he lives in
   By each and every choice he makes today.

And when all is said and done,
Mark's the only one
Who can make the world
A better place to stay.

3. I have lots of friends who call me names,
And that is the way they have to be.
But calling people names
Is just like playing games
And it really doesn't matter much to me.

[*chorus*]

Because I create the world I live in
By each and every choice I make today.
And whenever I say "Yes"
When I could have said "No,"
I make the world
A better place to stay.

The Boy
Who Lost His
Magic

I

THE boy stood quietly with his arms relaxed. There, barely discernible on a path leading out of the forest, was the silver wolf. Neither of them moved.

"How much longer can we wait?" asked the boy.

The wolf did not answer. He seemed to be sensing after something in the air. His powerful body was absolutely motionless.

"I'm not at all sure that I like this," the boy went on. "Everything is so—well, so different! Even *you* don't know what it's going to be like there. Or what is going to happen to us. Maybe we shouldn't go. Have you ever thought about that? About not going, I mean?"

The wolf was silent.

"How much longer can we wait?" asked the boy. There was no reply.

Then suddenly, wind. The silver wolf's fur stood on end. The boy shielded his eyes. Dead leaves swirled and scattered about his feet. The trees themselves seemed to be leaning over to touch him.

Now apparently the wolf was satisfied. He still didn't speak. Nor did he change his expression. But his muscles went slack and he turned completely around. For one desperate moment the boy thought of running away. But that moment ended, and then the three of them were headed down the path that led out of the forest. The silver wolf. The wind. And the boy who was soon to lose his magic.

II

His name was Joshua actually, but almost everybody called him Josh. His teacher often remarked that he was a pleasant enough child, if a bit unusual. Josh did not like school. He particularly disliked tracing letters of the alphabet onto lined paper. He was not very well coordinated anyway, and the task was just more than he could master. He liked to paint, but his style, while colorful, was that of utter abandon. Josh was frustrated. His teacher was puzzled. And the other children were less than gracious —especially when they learned that Josh traveled in the company of an imaginary wolf.

As far as the boy was concerned it had all been a mistake. They should never have left the forest in the first place. He longed to run beside the tiny brook, to roll in the leaves, to wrestle with his friend and then, exhausted, to lie in the warmth of the summer sun until his breath came back and they could begin again. Tracing letters onto lined paper, indeed! To begin with, what was the purpose of such an exercise? Even more confusing, why could no one understand that he had done it perfectly?

At first it surprised the boy that the other children could not see the silver wolf. Surely if they could see *him*, they could see the wolf! Such a strange predicament. But as time went on he came to accept the fact that he alone was aware of the magnificent animal's presence. He alone kept constant company with the silver wolf. The whole peculiar situation was terrifying to the boy. He admitted that he was frightened, and took comfort in the sustaining presence of the one the others could not see. Clearly they should never have left the forest in the first place, but at least he was not alone.

It is only if we remember that the boy and the wolf had been together forever prior to this time, and also that the wolf's presence now provided the only solace of his existence, that we can even begin to understand the gravity of what happened next. On Tuesday, October 23, in the morning, just after a group of the children had taken Simon's hat away from him at recess, Josh turned to speak with his friend. First he stared in disbelief, and then he screamed one long, agonized scream that echoed around the schoolyard. The silver wolf was gone.

III

Joshua stood quietly with his arms relaxed. For twenty-seven years now he had been searching for his friend. Over and over again he had described the silver wolf to startled travelers, wary shopkeepers, and indulgent academicians. Some expressed interest. Now and then an eyebrow was raised. But for the most part Joshua and his questions were received with a mixture of fascination and horror. Certainly the young man was crazy. Still, it was an intriguing story, and one found it difficult summarily to dismiss such an intense and passionate narrative. A silver wolf. That's what he had said. Has anyone seen a silver wolf? Again and again Joshua tried to describe his friend. But for all the good his efforts were to produce, he might as well have tried to describe the wind.

Every so often Joshua would think about Simon's hat. Perhaps it should be explained that this was what had provoked his turning to the wolf that tragic morning in October. The children had taken little Simon's hat and were playing catch with it. He was about to ask the wolf what sort of creature would delight in another's anguish, savor another's pain. What sort of creature would take Simon's hat away from him? He was about to ask the wolf all of this on Tuesday morning, October 23, in the schoolyard. His questions, of course, went unanswered. And so it was that twenty-seven years later, without yet having uncovered a single clue as to the wolf's whereabouts, Joshua found himself still thinking about Simon's hat.

That October, beginning on the anniversary of the wolf's disappearance, Joshua stood continually on a street corner of his sleepy village asking each person who passed by the same question.

"Why did you take Simon's hat?"

For awhile no one paid much attention to him. Before long, however, it became clear that this line of questioning was unnerving the citizenry. It was one thing to listen to his descriptions of the imaginary wolf, but it was quite another to be held accountable for such a trivial incident, especially when no one had any idea who Simon was, or when his hat had been taken! Joshua was urged to leave the street corner, but he would not go.

"Why," he asked angrily, "did you take Simon's hat?"

Sometime during the third month of this curious vigil the village citizens reached their breaking point. No one was ever able to explain the violent reaction to Joshua's continued questioning about Simon's hat. And there is probably little to be gained from further speculation. The point is, rather, that they did react violently. And that the good citizens of the village stoned Joshua to death right there on his street corner sometime near the end of the third month after his vigil had begun.

Perhaps Joshua had anticipated this action on the part of the citizenry. Perhaps not. In any case, it is clear that he was terrified at the moment of his full realization that they intended to kill him. Before the first stone was cast, Joshua closed his eyes and shrieked for the wolf. Then, when there was no response at all, he opened his eyes once again and was astonished to see that it was Simon who stood before him, a jagged rock in his left hand.

"They taught you this, Simon!" Joshua screamed. "They taught you this!" And then it was over.

Well, almost over. The good citizens of the village did not leave right away. For a short time they stared at Joshua's lifeless form and wondered why he had not gone home long before his death had become necessary. It was while they were asking themselves this and other such questions that Simon noticed a great silver wolf standing precisely on the spot where Joshua's body had been. Someone made an attempt to say something, but it was much too late. The snarling wolf's powerful body was already in the air, hurtling toward them.

Then suddenly, wind.

IV

The boy stood quietly with his arms relaxed. There, barely discernible on a path leading out of the forest, was the silver wolf. Neither of them moved.

"How much longer can we wait?" asked the boy.

On the Death of Colin Stuart

JESUS said to his disciples, "Ye now, therefore, have sorrow: but I will see you again, and your heart will rejoice, and your joy no man taketh from you."

He said: "Go now—have sorrow."

I. *Human beings do not belong to one another.* We are God's children. We belong to him. It is by sheer grace that we are together for a time—for a little while. We receive God's gift of another person in our lives with thanksgiving. But we must realize that this person is a gift—we cannot hang on, or refuse to let go of one of God's children when he calls.

II. *Colin Stuart was a gift. One of God's own tiny children.* And, for a time, God gave Colin to the world. In order that two human beings might have a child. And, later, in order that a woman might have a husband. And some children might have a father. And some other children might have a grandfather. For those children Colin defined what it means to have a father, or a grandfather. And a woman came to know what it means to have a husband. And because of Colin, the world understood more fully the greatness of the love of God. God loved the world so much that he gave it Colin. And that was nice of God.

III. *But now Colin Stuart is dead. And the world won't see him again. God took him back.* That's painful. And there is no way under heaven to minimize that pain. Jesus said, "Go now, therefore, and have sorrow." We do not sorrow because God is cruel or unjust. The world did nothing to deserve Colin. God gave him to us freely. Not because we deserved it, but because he loved us. We are not sorrowing because God is unjust. We are sorrowing because Colin is gone. And that's right. That's just right. Jesus said, "Go and have sorrow." A part of us is dead. That part of us that we called our father, or our grandfather, or our friend. That part of us we called Colin is gone. And we know the pain, and the emptiness, and the bitterness and the guilt, and the heartbreak all too well. We will never be the same. And that's right, too. We can't be "the same" ever again.

IV. *We are here to say good-bye to one of God's tiny children.* Jesus said, "Ye now, therefore, have sorrow: but I will see you again, and your heart will rejoice, and your joy no man taketh from you." He said, "When you pray, say 'Father.'" God loves Colin. And he belongs to him. He always has. For a time he gave him to the world. And now he has called him. And now we know emptiness. That's the way it is with human beings. We are here today, reluctantly, to offer Colin back to God. In so doing we are offering ourselves. We are here boldly—to dare to say "Our Father" and to pray "Thy will be done." We are here to trust God, and to love him, and to realize how much he loves us. We are here to say good-bye to Colin, one of God's tiny children. And today we must let go of his hand. But in so doing we give it over to that of his heavenly Father. We cannot hang on. We must let go. But God has hold of his hand. And he will never let go. Amen.

Wood
and Nails
and Colored Eggs

Wood

SOMETHING like an eternity ago, human beings got all caught up in the illusion that being human is a relatively unimportant sort of proposition. Here today—gone tomorrow. A vale of tears—that sort of foolishness.

What's more tragic, of course, is that in the wake of this basic error there quickly followed the idea that human beings are expendable, which easily degenerated into the proposition that some human beings are expendable. Certain human beings are expendable. Really bad guys are expendable. Guys with low I.Q.'s are expendable. Anyone who disagrees with me is expendable. A long time ago, human beings got all caught up in the illusion that being human is a relatively unimportant sort of proposition.

Well, that's not true. It's wrong. All wrong. And it has always been wrong. From the creation of the heavens and the earth, it has been—wrong. There is nothing more important than being human. Our lives have eternal significance. And no one—absolutely no one—is expendable.

Nails

Jesus was dead. He was dead and buried. It was expedient that he should be dead and buried. Caiaphas had explained that to himself and to others over and over again. It is expedient, he said, that one man should die for the sake of the people. Jesus is expendable. Caiaphas suffered from the illusion that being human is relatively unimportant. And so Jesus was dead.

What happened then wasn't so remarkable, really. God simply raised Jesus from the dead. He merely walked into the tomb that we call insignificance and absurdity, and meaninglessness, and other such names as that—he merely walked into this tomb and raised Jesus from the dead.

There was nothing very spectacular or remarkable about this. God revealed himself to be the same God who created the heavens and the earth and called his creation good; the same God who led his people out of Egypt to be a light to the nations; the same God who affirmed David in his weakness; who called forth the prophets; who kindled the heart of John the Baptist; and who reached out to touch his tiny children in the person of Jesus Christ.

God raised Jesus from the dead to the end that we should be clear—once and for all—that there is nothing more important than being human. Our lives have eternal significance. And no one—absolutely no one—is expendable.

Colored Eggs

Some human beings are fortunate enough to be able to color eggs on Easter. If you have a pair of hands to hold the eggs, or if you are fortunate enough to be able to see the brilliant colors, then you are twice blessed.

This Easter some of us cannot hold the eggs, others of us cannot see the colors, many of us are unable to move at all—and so it will be necessary to color eggs in our hearts.

This Easter there is a hydrocephalic child lying very still in a hospital bed nearby with a head the size of his pillow and vacant, unmoving eyes, and he will not be able to color Easter eggs, and he will not be able to color Easter eggs in his heart, and so God will have to color eggs for him.

And God will color eggs for him. You can bet your life and the life of the created universe on that.

At the cross of Calvary God reconsecrated and sanctified wood and nails and absurdity and helplessness to be continuing vehicles of his love. And then he simply raised Jesus from the dead. And they both went home and colored eggs.

COME GATHER, CHILDREN

Come ga - ther, chil - dren ev - ery - where. Come and

lis - ten.___ Come and see. It is God a - lone who

gives us our lives, And God who sets us free.

Free to live. Free to de - cide. To

make our world what it will be. And

then it is God who de - mands that we die. And that's

just   the   way   it   is   for   you   and   me.   And

God likes me just   the   way   I   am.   I   turned out   just

right.   But   I'll   sing   it   a - gain   in

case   I   for - get.   And, strange as   it   seems, I   might.

COME GATHER, CHILDREN

1. Come gather, children everywhere.
   Come and listen. Come and see.
   It is God alone who gives us our lives,
   And God who sets us free.
   Free to live. Free to decide.
   To make our world what it will be.
   And then it is God who demands that we die.
   And that's just the way it is for you and me.

   And God likes me just the way I am.
   I turned out just right.
   But I'll sing it again in case I forget.
   And, strange as it seems, I might.

2. If God is the One who gives us our lives,
   Then children of God we must be.
   But how can we be children of someone we can't
      hold?
   Of a Father we can't see?
   And God can't be held. And God can't be seen.
   But we meet Him whenever we're set free.
   And we learn about freedom when we learn the
      way life is,
   And that you and I decide how it will be.

And God likes me just the way I am.
I turned out just right.
But I'll sing it again in case I forget.
And, strange as it seems, I might.

3. Come gather, children everywhere.
   Come and listen. Come and see.
   It is God alone who gives us our lives,
   And God who sets us free.
   Free to live. Free to decide.
   To make our world what it will be.
   And then it is God who demands that we die.
   And that's just the way it is for you and me.

   And God likes me just the way I am.
   I turned out just right.
   But I'll sing it again in case I forget.
   And, strange as it seems, I might.

   And God likes me just the way I am.
   I turned out just right.
   But I'll sing it again in case I forget.
   And, strange as it seems, I might.

Rag-Tag
Army

I THINK God must be very old and very tired.
Maybe he used to look splendid and fine in his general's uniform, but no more. He's been on the march
a long time, you know. And look at his rag-tag little
army! All he has for soldiers are you and me. Dumb
little army. Listen! The drum beat isn't even regular.
Everyone is out of step. And there! You see? God
keeps stopping along the way to pick up one of his
tinier soldiers who decided to wander off and play
with a frog, or run in a field, or whose foot got tangled
in the underbrush. He'll never get anywhere that
way. And yet, the march goes on.

Do you see how the marchers have broken up
into little groups? Look at that group up near the
front. Now, there's a snappy outfit. They all look
pretty much alike—at least they're in step with each
other. That's something! Only they're not wearing
their shoes. They're carrying them in their hands. Silly
little band. They won't get far before God will have
to stop again.

Or how about that other group over there?
They're all holding hands as they march. The only
trouble with this is the men on each end of the line.

Pretty soon they realize that one of their hands isn't holding onto anything—one hand is reaching, empty, alone. And so they hold hands with each other, and everybody marches around in circles. The more people holding hands, the bigger the circle. And, of course, a bigger circle is deceptive because as we march along it looks like we're going someplace, but we're not. And so God must stop again. You see what I mean? He'll never get anywhere that way!

If God were more sensible he'd take his little army and shape them up. Why, whoever heard of a soldier stopping to romp in a field? It's ridiculous. But even more absurd is a general who will stop the march of eternity to go and bring him back. But that's God for you. His is no endless, empty marching. He is going somewhere. His steps are deliberate and purposive. He may be old, and he may be tired. But he knows where he's going. And he means to take every last one of his tiny soldiers with him. Only there aren't going to be any forced marches. And, after all, there are frogs and flowers, and thorns and underbrush along the way. And even though our foreheads have been signed with the sign of the cross, we are only human. And most of us are afraid and lonely and would like to hold hands or cry or run away. And we don't know where we are going, and we can't seem to trust God—especially when it's dark out and we can't see him! And he won't go on without us. And that's why it's taking so long.

Listen! The drum beat isn't even regular. Everyone is out of step. And there! You see? God keeps stopping along the way to pick up one of his tinier soldiers who decided to wander off and play with a frog, or run in a field, or whose foot got tangled in the underbrush. He'll never get anywhere that way!

And yet, the march goes on. . . .

The Wheat and the Tares

THE Kingdom of God, Lord, is like so many things. Yet like nothing at all that I have ever known. Perhaps my poor head will never even grasp a single strand from your complex multiplicity of images. But the story about the wheat and the tares will always be hardest of all for me to understand. Because, at the end, the man burns the tares. And if the tares represent people, Lord, I'll never understand that. Never.

The Kingdom of God is like so many things. Did you mean for the wheat to represent good people, Lord? And are the tares then desperate and evil men whose willful sins are so bound to them that there is no release—only the fire? And is it somehow a stranger who stands responsible, after all? (I mean ultimately responsible, since it is he who has sown the tares in the first place.) Is this what the story means, Lord? That God created good men? And that somehow a stranger brought into being a number of bad men? And that the good men and the bad men must continue to live together side by side until the day of judgment when they will be either rewarded or punished? God, I hope that's not what the story means. Partly because I am an evil and desperate man. More because I am willfully an evil and desperate man. Heard this way, the story promises me nothing but the fire. Lord, will there be nothing for me but the fire?

The Kingdom of God is like so many things. Yet like nothing at all that I have ever known. For there is no godliness in my daily walks amidst the meaningless drudgery of my life. There is only disappointment. And, at that, hardly any large-scale, dramatic, or bitter let-down. Only the simple, weary disappointment that is certainly the most disturbing by-product of any real insight. My world has disappointed me. I have disappointed myself. Lord help me to understand. Could it be the very fabric of existence itself that is permeated by tares? Dare I hope that all of mankind is represented by the wheat and that it is in explanation of the distortion of life itself that the parable is told? Is it impudent of me to wonder whether or not you are referring to the very stuff of existence as having been somehow corrupted; with the corresponding result that all men find themselves living in a matrix of sin and of desperation and of disappointment? Is it only I, Lord? Or do all men find themselves inextricably in the grasp of meaninglessness and sin? Dare I hope that the tares do not represent people, but rather alienation and despair, the universal condition of existing men? Have I misunderstood the parable, Lord? Or have I misunderstood the Kingdom of God?

The Kingdom of God is like so many things. I

hope that the parable of the wheat and the tares is about man's universal condition of sinfulness and alienation. I pray, Lord, that in the end it will be this alienation that is destroyed and the whole of mankind that is gathered into the Kingdom. If so, then there is no longer any mystery as to the identity of the stranger who sowed the seeds. He is none other than I, myself. And there comes to my conscious awareness a new appreciation for the old saying that I am my own worst enemy. We have each of us sown the tares, and we are all of us virtually strangled by them. If this is what you are telling us, Lord, burn the tares that we have sown in order that mankind may breathe! Burn the tares and gather your children into the Kingdom. I hope that's what you meant by the parable of the wheat and the tares, Lord. I believe that's what you meant. I'm betting my life that's what you meant. But if the tares represent people, Lord, then you are the stranger. Because at the end the man burns the tares. And if the tares represent people, Lord, I'll never understand that. Never. Amen.

Now, Therefore, Tiger

Now, therefore, tiger.
Voluptuous, feline beast from
      God knows what
            forbidden place.
A burning, scowling echo
      stalking silently;
      embracing
            Men who long ago
      resigned themselves
            to history,
            and hopelessness,
            and fate.
What then? Will it be this most
      terrible of beasts
      who finally penetrates
The long abandoned corridors
      of courage,
            and replaces
      all our nameless fears with joy?
It will, indeed.
      Yet do not be deceived.
            The tiger
    comes

to shatter
and destroy.
Now, therefore, tiger.
The time of celebration is at hand.
Prepare the wedding feast.
The bridegroom crouches
motionless
outside the door
and licks his fangs.
One might at least plead ignorance
or
something of the kind.
God! Anything at all to
buy some time,
some breathing space,
some room.
A momentary solitude, perhaps.
Damn everything.
The tiger comes too soon.
Monstrous cat! Go back to that
mysterious,
hidden place
from which
you came.
Now quickly, we must turn the lock
and bolt the door.
Let no one even dare
to speak his name.
So there. The tiger's safely
sealed within our tomb.
A captive of

anxiety,
despair, and
fate.
           And yet,
what mad presumption to assume that
           such a creature
could be conquered by
A state of separation
       quite so coarse and unrefined
       as that of death.
This present flexing of his muscles
       gives the lie
                 to what is left
Of my belief that he is subject
       to the tomb
       or, shall I say,
                 to anything
                 or anyone
                 at all
       except, perhaps,
       the silver wolf himself.
Now, therefore, tiger.
The time of celebration is at hand.
       Prepare the feast.
                 The bridegroom crouches
       motionless
       outside the door
                 and licks his fangs.
Yet what in God's name
                 does he want with me?
       My death, no doubt.

But
can't he see
That's absolutely all
I have to give—
except my wooden spoon,
a panda bear,
and
an uncommon love
For one peculiar child?
Truth to tell,
I do not think
I'll ever understand
the tiger's
strategy
and plan.
I am consigned to
stand and wait.
Perhaps
that's
just as well.

Counterquestion

THERE he is. In the temple again. Causing trouble. Speaking very differently from other preachers. Speaking with authority about sorrow, anxiety, sickness and death. Penetrating the darkest corners of human existence. Shattering illusion. Make no mistake about it; this is a dangerous man.

The Christ Event. Jesus of Nazareth. The man for others, whose words cut through our most stubborn defenses and expose the whole of humanity in its nakedness. The fugitive who confronts us with direct authority. The one in whose presence the lame rise up and walk. The poor are comforted. The eyes of the blind are opened. The diseased are healed. Who would dare even to speak his name for fear of the consequences?

But now as he comes into the temple, the chief priests and the elders of the people approach him and say, "By what authority are you doing these things?" Have they no fear at all? No sense of the mystery?

For a moment Jesus is silent. Only his eyes betray impatience. Then suddenly a counterquestion: "What do you think about John the Baptist? Was he the instrument of God in history or a charlatan?"

The question is disturbing and exceedingly difficult to answer. John the Baptist is considered by the
general populace to have been a prophet. It would
be easier to reply that John was the instrument of
God in history—not a charlatan in any sense. The
problem with this answer is that Jesus will immediately ask why they did not repent and believe what
John had said. On the other hand, to say that John
was a charlatan would be to incur the wrath of the
people.

The chief priests and the elders will not risk
either answer. The compromise that they decide upon
is to say, "Who knows? Who knows whether John
was the instrument of God or a charlatan? We can't
say!"

Jesus doesn't even look at them. Now he is ready
to answer their question about authority. "Who
knows?" he says. "Who knows by what authority
I do these things? I can't say!"

The chief priests deserve that. The elders should
have known better than to ask the question in the
first place. If they are not willing to risk themselves,
what difference will it make what Jesus says?

Instead of answering the chief priests and the
elders directly, Jesus asks a counterquestion. If his
assailants admit that John the Baptist acted and
preached on divine authority, then they must be
prepared to reorder their lives according to what John
had called for. That is to say, they must commit
themselves. If, on the other hand, they believe that
John was a fanatic and a charlatan, they must be

prepared to say so—no matter how unpopular such an opinion might be. Once again, to answer the question implies commitment.

For timid and cautious men who are unwilling to take the risk involved in either answer, the only possible response is, "Who knows?"

But then, what is there left for Jesus to say? We do not know the Christ and then commit ourselves to him. Commitment is the one and only way by which we may know the Christ.

There he is. In the temple again. Causing trouble. Tearing away the shroud that surrounds careful and frightened men who have come to accept disillusionment as a way of life. Cutting to the heart of those who dare not trust anything or anyone until they are certain that this trust will not be violated. Holding up the absolute necessity of deciding before the lives of men who would prefer to remain on the sidelines as spectators and onlookers. Challenging the chief priests and the elders to adopt a responsible position, regardless of what it is! The Christ Event. Jesus of Nazareth. The man for others.

What do you think of John the Baptist? Was he God's instrument in history, or a charlatan? They have just fifteen seconds to decide.

What the chief priests and the elders do not realize is that life itself is inextricably bound to decision making. To live is to decide, to risk being wrong, to bet your life. Nothing could be more foreign to the ears of these analytical men who have come to observe the young man from Nazareth. Yet nothing could be more central to their understanding of what he is all about.

By what authority is he doing these things? That is the question. Good! But the deeper puzzle that must first be untangled is why they want to know anyway! What difference will it make? What risks are they prepared to take? Is this question really one of final seriousness for them? How ready are they to commit themselves before God?

And so, the counterquestion. What about John the Baptist? Prophet or madman?

To live is to decide, to risk being wrong, to bet your life. Life itself is inextricably bound to decision making. It is not enough to be interested in this man, or fascinated by him or drawn to him. Either we stand ready to commit our deaths to him or we don't. No one ever knows the Christ and then commits himself. Commitment is the one and only way by which we may know the Christ.

By what authority is he doing these things? What do you think? Is he the one to whom all power in heaven and on earth is given, or is he an invented dream of human longing?

Yes or no? To live is to decide, to risk being wrong. It is not enough to be interested in, or fascinated by Jesus of Nazareth. It is not enough to be frightened, cautious, and bewildered spectators. Curiosity about the Christ Event in history is not enough. Either we stand ready to commit our deaths or we don't.

Actually, it shouldn't be all that frightening.

Everyone has to die anyway. It's not as if there were some other option. Each of us must die. That's a given. That's just the way it is. What is not part of the given is the how, or the why, or the what for of your death. What you are going to die for is not a given. What your death is going to be about is up to you.

So what do you think? By what authority is he doing these things? The chief priests and the elders will not risk themselves. It is clear that they are not really serious about wanting to know. Although they are interested in Jesus, even fascinated by him, the ecclesiastical dignitaries are not ready to commit their deaths to anything or anyone.

But what about you? What is your answer? It's all very well to say, "God knows!" But such an evasion cannot suffice. God never has to decide. Men do.

There he is. In the temple again. Causing trouble. The broken one who cuts through our most stubborn defenses and demands that we place our lives on the line. The fugitive who confronts us with direct authority. Make no mistake about it; this is a dangerous man.

BRAND OF THE TIGER

I'll wear the brand of the ti - ger _____ And

while I'm a - live I'll be free. I'll stalk this land like a ti - ger _

Mile af - ter mile 'til I see The life _ that was in-tend-ed, _____

_____ When bro-ken hearts are mend-ed _____ And war at last is

end - ed _____ That time will sure - ly be. _____

Words and music copyright © 1970 by Martin Bell

BRAND OF THE TIGER

I'll wear the brand of the tiger
And while I'm alive I'll be free.
I'll stalk this land like a tiger
Mile after mile 'til I see
The life that was intended,
When broken hearts are mended
And war at last is ended—
That time will surely be.

I'll wear the brand of the tiger
And while I'm alive I'll be free;
Wild as a storm on the ocean
A child of the wind and the sea.
A fool who's born to wander,
I'll learn to speak like thunder.
But now and then I wonder
What will become of me?

Guileless and naked the tiger
Childlike and open and free.
I'll stalk this land like a tiger
Mile after mile 'til I see
The life that was intended,

When broken hearts are mended
And war at last is ended—
That time will surely be.

I'll wear the brand of the tiger
And while I'm alive I'll be free;
Wild as a storm on the ocean
A child of the wind and the sea.
A fool who's born to wander,
I'll learn to speak like thunder.
But now and then I wonder
What will become of me?

The Porcupine
Whose Name
Didn't Matter

JOGGI stood before the mystery of his own life much
as any other porcupine might have. That is to say,
he was exceedingly cautious in the face of it. I do not
mean to imply that it was difficult for Joggi to ac-
knowledge the mystery. On the contrary! He had
no trouble whatsoever recognizing the ebb and
flow of his own limitations and the infinite variety
and possibility within his universe. Joggi knew about
the ongoing beat of life. The daily. The humdrum.
The having-one-day-showed-up; and now, like it or
not, the finding-oneself-here in the midst of existence, virtually crushed by an environment, called
upon to create the entire world; the bittersweet
mingling of all of this with an inner insistence to go
on, and on, until. . . . Until what? Joggi knew about
the ongoing beat of life. It throbbed somewhere deep
within him. Beneath the prickly spines. In the center
of his tiny body. A thumping. Steady. Insistent. Unrelenting. The mystery.

  Totally aware, more lucid perhaps than he de-
sired to be, Joggi lived and loved, laughed and cried
—tentatively. One might say that anger, frustration
and tenderness had been so delicately woven into the

fabric of his person as to make difficult our perceiving any of them.

Joggi was cautious in the face of the mystery. So cautious, in fact, that almost nobody knew his name. Most of the animals in the forest had seen the near-sighted porcupine moving slowly about, poking his pointed black nose into the vegetation, bristling and puffing, squinting and stumbling. Few had spoken to him. Now and then someone would say hello, and ask after his health—an attempt to strike up a conversation of sorts. This never really led to anything, however, because Joggi would not—no, that isn't fair—Joggi could not risk such a head-on collision.

Joggi's decisional hesitancy usually expressed itself this way. When asked what his name was, he would answer, "It doesn't matter! It doesn't matter what my name is! Can't you see? What difference does it make? I won't tell you what my name is, because it doesn't matter!"

That would be the reply. And, more often than not, that would be the end of the conversation. Joggi could not embrace another, he would not tell anyone his name, and the result was almost always the same: the other animals avoided him.

One significant exception to this was Gamiel, the raccoon. Gamiel did not mind Joggi's reticence at all. It did not bother him when the prickly little porcupine was silent for hours at a time, and he had never even thought to ask about Joggi's name.

Gamiel could remember very little before the accident, and much of what had happened since was blurred somewhere in the recesses of his brain, all but lost to memory.

Raccoons are generally alert and resourceful creatures with keen perceptions and excellent memories. But all of this had changed for Gamiel. Ironically, he wasn't even certain why. There had been a flash of light, and then something hard ripped into the side of his head. His whole body convulsed with the pain; white hot, wet, thrashing, God-when-will-it-stop pain that pitched him bleeding from the tree into the underbrush and drove him forward without his left side pulling any weight at all, by instinct only; screaming pain that shrieked behind his eyes the one and only word of hope he knew, and then, as suddenly as it had come, was gone.

Gamiel had only to look at himself in the quiet waters of the forest pond to recognize why no one would come near him anymore. Everything had changed. He did not even look like a raccoon. The whole left side of his head was missing, he had no fur at all around his eyes where once the elegant mask had been, and he could barely pull himself along with his right front leg. Gamiel had only to look at himself in the forest pond to realize why everyone hurried past when he called out to them.

But the crippled raccoon never again would look at his reflection in the quiet waters. Not because he wasn't willing to see his disfigured image, but rather because he wasn't able to see anything at all. Ever since the accident, Gamiel had been totally blind.

Joggi found Gamiel about two days after the

pain had stopped, and approximately three hours after the raccoon had given up all hope.

A sound close by. Gamiel trembled.

"Is someone there?" he whispered.

At first Joggi didn't say anything. He looked at Gamiel and noted that his left side was paralyzed. Then, after a moment, he realized that the animal was blind. The nearsighted porcupine moved closer.

"You're a raccoon," he said out loud.

"Oh, yes, indeed I am!" Gamiel stuttered. "Only I think something awful has happened to me. I cannot see anything at all, and I can barely move. Please, tell me what has happened to me! Am I going to die? Why won't anyone stop when I cry out? Why can't I see? What has happened? Please . . . I'm afraid. . . ." And in Gamiel's searching, empty, sightless eyes tears began to form.

Joggi sniffed. In the center of his body the beat of life. Faster now. Answer him. Don't just stand there with your spines bristling and your heart pounding. Answer him!

Joggi spoke with a steady and quiet voice.

"I believe you have been shot. I cannot be certain, of course, but that is my opinion. Are you in a great deal of pain?"

"No. At first there was pain. But I can't feel anything now. In fact, my whole left side is numb. No. No more pain. Just, well . . . nothing." Gamiel's eyes opened and closed aimlessly.

Joggi was silent. His tiny body shivering; breathing labored, short difficult breaths. What now? An extended period of time.

Gamiel spoke in a hoarse voice, "Are you still there?"

Joggi's heart beat faster. "Yes, I'm here. I was just wondering what to do now."

"Oh, you don't have to do anything! Honestly, I mean that! You don't have to do anything at all. Just stay with me for a little while. Just be there. Just don't go away. Please. You don't have to do anything! Just stay with me. I'm afraid! You won't go away, will you?"

Joggi swallowed hard. "No," he said deliberately and with as much conviction as he could muster, "no, I won't go away."

"Thank you," Gamiel said quietly. And then the wounded raccoon fell asleep.

Joggi stood beside Gamiel all that day. Then when evening came, a cool breeze made his spines whistle slightly. The sound woke the raccoon.

"Are you there?"

"Yes. I told you I wouldn't go away."

"I'm hungry."

"I thought you probably would be," Joggi replied. "Can you move at all?"

Gamiel stretched his right leg forward and pulled himself along the ground.

"Good for you!" said Joggi. "That will do nicely. I can bring you food, but you will need to maneuver for yourself in order to get water. I believe you have enough strength to reach the pond; it isn't very far, and I can guide you directly to it. Come on. Let's see how it goes."

That was how it began. An unusual partnership, perhaps. Certainly the rest of the animals in the forest were surprised to see the pair of them moving slowly about, managing to live from one day to the next without really doing much of anything. Occasionally Joggi would describe something for Gamiel, or answer a question, or direct the crippled raccoon toward a tasty morsel of food. Gamiel, for his part, chattered happily, basked in the sun, and generally enjoyed his friend's company.

They made a home for one another, Joggi and Gamiel. Not a regular home exactly; not a place. More like a shelter from the excessive pain that each of them had known. A coming together of two lonely and frightened creatures. A bond of trust that asked no questions, expected nothing at all except the merciful being together that made waking up tomorrow possible. Gamiel didn't mind when Joggi was silent for hours at a time. He could sense the beat. Thumping, ongoing, steady. There. It was enough.

Joggi was with Gamiel for one full year before the injured raccoon finally died. It was a quiet event, almost a surprise but that Joggi had been expecting it for so long. Gamiel's strength just finally gave out and the mystery enveloped him completely.

"You know, I've been expecting this for quite some time now," Joggi said to the raccoon who lay there on the ground, no longer able to hear him.

"I am surprised that you managed to stay alive as long as you did. I knew the day that I found you it couldn't last. Not for long. You'd been hurt too badly. I never expected you to live this long. And yet . . . well, I hoped that it might have been a little longer. Do you know what I mean? You see, I never knew anybody very well before. Not that we ever talked much, or anything like that. But I felt like I knew you anyway. Even without talking. I have a really hard time talking to anybody, or getting to know anybody. And nobody ever wants to get very close to me because of all these spines that I have sticking out of me. I don't suppose you ever knew that I had spines sticking out all over me, did you? They're sort of like needles and they're sharp. I guess they scare everybody a bit. I hope you don't mind my talking so much. I really don't know why I'm talking to you now. I suppose it's just that I had a little more to tell you before you died; I have been wanting to say this for almost a year and never quite found the right time to do it. It's too late now, I realize, but I've been wanting to tell you that it has been an honor to meet you, and that you are indeed a very handsome raccoon, and that I would like to consider you my friend."

The porcupine cleared his throat. A tear dropped onto his nose. In the center of his body the ongoing beat of life. Beneath the prickly spines. Wildly thumping. Tell him! Don't just stand there with your spines bristling and your heart pounding. Tell him!

Some Gospel Themes

Then the righteous will reply, "Lord, when was it that we saw you hungry and fed you, or thirsty and gave you drink, a stranger and took you home, or naked and clothed you? When did we see you ill or in prison, and come to visit you?" And the king will answer, "I tell you this: anything you did for one of my brothers here, however humble, you did for me." *Matthew 25:37–40*

Jesus answered, "Foxes have their holes, the birds their [nests]; but the Son of Man has nowhere to lay his head." *Luke 9:58*

With the crowds swarming round him he went on to say: "This is a wicked generation. It demands a sign, and the only sign that will be given it is the sign of Jonah. For just as Jonah was a sign to the Ninevites, so will the Son of Man be to this generation." *Luke 11:29–30*

"By gaining his life a man will lose it; by losing his for my sake, he will gain it." *Matthew 10:39*

At that time the disciples came to Jesus and asked, "Who is the greatest in the kingdom of Heaven?" He called a child, set him in front of them, and said, "I tell you this: unless you turn round and become like children, you will never enter the kingdom of Heaven. Let a man humble himself till he is like this child, and he will be the greatest in the kingdom of Heaven. Whoever receives one such child in my name receives me. But if a man is a cause of stumbling to one of these little ones who have faith in me, it would be better for him to have a millstone hung round his neck and be drowned in the depths of the sea. Alas for the world that such causes of stumbling arise! Come they must, but woe betide the man through whom they come!" *Matthew 18:1–7*

Some time later Jesus withdrew to the farther shore of the Sea of Galilee (or Tiberias), and a large crowd of people followed who had seen the signs he performed in healing the sick. Then Jesus went up the hillside and sat down with his disciples. It was near the time of Passover, the great Jewish festival. Raising his eyes and seeing a large crowd coming towards him, Jesus said to Philip, "Where are we to buy bread to feed these people?" This he said to test him; Jesus himself knew what he meant to do. Philip replied, "Twenty pounds would not buy enough bread for every one of them to have a little." One of his disciples, Andrew, the brother of Simon Peter, said to him, "There is a boy here who has five barley loaves and two fishes; but what is that among so many?" Jesus said, "Make the people sit down." There was plenty of grass there, so the men sat down, about five thousand of them. Then Jesus took the loaves, gave thanks, and distributed them to the people as they sat there. He did the same with the fishes, and they had as much as they wanted. When everyone had had enough, he said to his disciples, "Collect the pieces left over, so that nothing may be lost." This they did, and filled twelve baskets with the pieces left uneaten of the five barley loaves. *John 6:1–13*

As he was entering a village he was met by ten men with leprosy. They stood some way off and called out to him, "Jesus, Master, take pity on us." When he saw them he said, "Go and show yourselves to the priests"; and while they were on their way, they were made clean. One of them, finding himself cured, turned back praising God aloud. He threw himself down at Jesus's feet and thanked him. And he was a Samaritan. At this Jesus said: "Were not all ten cleansed? The other nine, where are they? Could none be found to come back and give praise to God except this foreigner?" And he said to the man, "Stand up and go on your way; your faith has cured you." *Luke 17:12–19*

Now there was a man in the synagogue possessed by an unclean spirit. He shrieked: "What do you want with us, Jesus of Nazareth? Have you come to destroy us? I know who you are—the Holy One of God." Jesus rebuked him: "Be silent," he said, "and come out of him." And the unclean spirit threw the man into convulsions and with a loud cry left him. They were all dumbfounded and began to ask one another, "What is this? A new kind of teaching! He speaks with authority. When he gives orders, even the unclean spirits submit." The news spread rapidly, and he was soon spoken of all over the district of Galilee. *Mark 1:23–28*

". . . you shall know the truth, and the truth will set you free." *John 8:32*

"Be ready for action, with belts fastened and lamps alight. Be like men who wait for their master's return from a wedding-party, ready to let him in the moment he arrives and knocks. Happy are those servants whom the master finds on the alert when he comes. I tell you this: he will fasten his belt, seat them at table, and come and wait on them. Even if it is the middle of the night or before dawn when he comes, happy they if he finds them alert. And remember, if the householder had known what time the burglar was coming he would not have let his house be broken into. Hold yourselves ready, then, because the Son of Man will come at the time you least expect him." *Luke 12:35–40*

When all things began, the Word already was.

The Word dwelt with God, and what God was, the Word was. *John 1:1*

Jesus answered, "Have I been all this time with you, Philip, and you still do not know me? Anyone who has seen me has seen the Father. Then how can you say, 'Show us the Father'? Do you not believe that I am in the Father, and the Father in me? I am not myself the source of the words I speak to you: it is the Father who dwells in me doing his own work. Believe me when I say that I am in the Father and the Father in me; or else accept the evidence of the deeds themselves. In truth, in very truth I tell you, he who has faith in me will do what I am doing; and he will do greater things still because I am going to the Father." *John 14:9–12*

He brought Simon to Jesus, who looked at him and said, "You are Simon son of John. You shall be called Cephas" (that is, Peter, the Rock). *John 1:42*

"Are not sparrows five for twopence? And yet not one of them is overlooked by God. More than that, even the hairs of your head have all been counted. Have no fear; you are worth more than any number of sparrows." *Luke 12:6–7*

He also said to them, "The Sabbath was made for the sake of man and not man for the Sabbath." *Mark 2:27*

"Is there a man among you who will offer his son a stone when he asks for bread, or a snake when he asks for fish? If you, then, bad as you are, know how to give your children what is good for them, how much more will your heavenly Father give good things to those who ask him!" *Matthew 7:9–11*

He came to the disciples and found them asleep; and he said to Peter, "What! Could none of you stay awake with me one hour? Stay awake, and pray that you may be spared the test. The spirit is willing, but the flesh is weak." *Matthew 26:40–41*

"I am to stay no longer in the world, but they are still in the world, and I am on my way to thee. Holy Father, protect by the power of thy name those whom thou hast given me, that they may be one, as we are one." *John 17:11*

A man sowed his field with good seed; but while everyone was asleep his enemy came, sowed [tares] among the wheat, and made off. When the corn sprouted and began to fill out, the [tares] could be seen among it. The farmer's men went to their master and said, "Sir, was it not good seed that you sowed in your field? Then where has the [tare] come from?" "This is an enemy's doing," he replied. "Well then," they said, "shall we go and gather the [tares]?" "No," he answered; "in gathering it you might pull up the wheat at the same time. Let them both grow together till harvest; and at harvest-time I will tell the reapers, 'Gather the [tares] first, and tie it in bundles for burning; then collect the wheat into my barn.'" *Matthew 13:24–30*

He entered the temple, and the chief priests and elders of the nation came to him with the question: "By what authority are you acting like this? Who gave you this authority?" Jesus replied, "I have a question to ask you too; answer it, and I will tell you by what authority I act. The baptism of John: was it from God, or from men?" This set them arguing among themselves: "If we say, 'from God,' he will say, 'Then why did you not believe him?' But if we say, 'from men,' we are afraid of the people, for they all take John for a prophet." So they answered, "We do not know." And Jesus said: "Then neither will I tell you by what authority I act." *Matthew 21:23–27*

"To receive you is to receive me, and to receive me is to receive the One who sent me. Whoever receives a prophet as a prophet will be given a prophet's reward, and whoever receives a good man because he is a good man will be given a good man's reward. And if anyone gives so much as a cup of cold water to one of these little ones, because he is a disciple of mine, I tell you this: that man will assuredly not go unrewarded." *Matthew 10:40–42*